A Woman's Workshop on ROMANS

Books in this series—

Behold Your God: A Woman's Workshop on the Attributes of God
    With suggestions for leaders
    by Myrna Alexander

A Woman's Workshop on Faith
    Student's Manual
    Leader's Manual
    by Martha Hook

A Woman's Workshop on James
    With Suggestions for Leaders
    by Carolyn Nystrom and Margaret Fromer

A Woman's Workshop on Proverbs
    Student's Manual
    Leader's Manual
    by Diane Bloem

A Woman's Workshop on Bible Marriages
    Student's Manual
    Leader's Manual
    by Diane Bloem and Robert C. Bloem

A Woman's Workshop on Mastering Motherhood
    With suggestions for leaders
    by Barbara Bush

A Woman's Workshop on Romans
    Student's Manual
    Leader's Manual
    by Carolyn Nystrom

Our Life Together: A Woman's Workshop on Fellowship
    With suggestions for leaders
    by Larry Richards

A Woman's Workshop on the Beatitudes
    Student's Manual/Leader's Manual
    by Diane Bloem

A Woman's Workshop on ROMANS

Carolyn Nystrom

Student's Manual

ZONDERVAN PUBLISHING HOUSE OF THE ZONDERVAN CORPORATION
GRAND RAPIDS, MICHIGAN 49506

Scripture passages are quoted from *The New International Version,*
Copyright © 1978 by The New York International Bible Society.

A WOMAN'S WORKSHOP ON ROMANS—Student's Manual*
Copyright © 1981 by The Zondervan Corporation
Grand Rapids, Michigan

Second printing January 1982

*Adapted from *Romans: Christianity on Trial,* Carolyn Nystrom, Harold Shaw Publishers, 1980.

ISBN 0-310-41921-2

Edited and designed by Louise H. Rock.

Printed in the United States of America

CONTENTS

THE BOOK OF ROMANS

Paul's letter to the Romans presents more clearly than any other book of Scripture a thorough defense of the Christian faith. It's as if Christianity were a tree. Paul points out its roots in God's covenant with Abraham, its massive trunk in the life and death of Jesus Christ, and branches of faith that extend into all areas of daily experience. Inhabitants of the twentieth century need this kind of aerial view of Christianity.

At the same time, Paul does not gloss over sticky details. He treats such old bugaboos as "Are the heathen lost?" and "If God knows I can't stop sinning, why should I try?" with the same care as he does the large perspective. He interweaves these critical questions into the total scheme of Christian theology, strengthening each part with careful attention to every small thread. Since questions of these same details often shake our faith, Romans is doubly appropriate.

Paul addresses the church in Rome, a church he had not visited personally but which contained friends he had met in his journeys through Greece and Asia. Since Paul knew it would be some time before he could come to the church (in fact it was three years) he wrote down in orderly fashion the whole framework of Christian teaching. Because of this letter, Paul hoped that when he eventually saw his Roman friends, they could be "mutually encouraged by each other's faith."

We, Paul's twentieth century readers, are the beneficiaries of his loving concern for a church he had never seen. Like the Romans, we need a clear picture of what we believe, and why, and how these beliefs relate to those of the rest of the world. Like the Romans, we need to bring order to the way we live because of our faith. And because God promises eternal life to those who accept these teachings, we, with the Romans, may someday greet the apostle Paul in person.

I'VE JOINED THE GROUP. NOW WHAT?

You've joined a group of people willing to admit that the Bible is worth studying. Some will admit to far more than that—that the Bible is the Word of God and therefore a standard for day-to-day decisions. Others may say that the Bible is merely a collection of interesting teachings and tales, worthy of time and interest but not much more. You may place yourself at one end of this spectrum, or you may fit somewhere in the middle. But you have one goal in common with those in your group: You believe that the Bible is worth your time, and you hope to enjoy studying it together.

To meet this goal, a few simple guidelines will prevent needless problems.

1. **Take a Bible with you.** Any modern translation is fine. Suggested versions include: *Revised Standard Version, New American Standard Bible, Today's English Version, New International Version, Jerusalem Bible.*

A few versions, however, do not work well in group Bible study. For beautiful language, the *King James Version* is unsurpassed. Yours may bear great sentimental value because it belonged to your grandmother. But if you use a *King James*, you will spend a great deal of effort translating the Elizabethan English into today's phrasing, perhaps losing valuable meaning in the process.

Paraphrases like *Living Bible, Phillips,* and *Amplified* are especially helpful in private devotions, but they lack the accuracy of a translation by Bible scholars. Therefore leave these at home on Bible study day.

If you would like to match the phrasing of the questions in this guide, use the *New International Version*. However, if you fear that any Bible is far too difficult for you to understand, try *Today's English Version*. This easy-to-read translation is certain to change your mind.

2. **Arrive at Bible study on time.** You'll feel as if you're half a step behind throughout the entire session if you miss the Bible reading and the opening survey questions.

3. **Call your hostess if you are going to be absent.** This saves her setting a place for you if refreshments are served. It also frees the group to begin on time without waiting needlessly for you.

4. **Volunteer to be a hostess.** A quick way to feel as if you belong is to have the Bible study group meet at your house.

5. **Decide if you are a talker or a listener.** This is a discussion Bible study, and for a discussion to work well all persons should participate more or less equally.

If you are a talker, before you speak count ten after the leader asks the question. Try waiting until several other people speak before you give your own point of view. If you're a listener, remind yourself that just as you benefit from what others say, they profit from your ideas. Besides, your insights will mean more even to you if you put them into words and say them out loud. So take courage and speak.

6. **Keep on track.** This is a group responsibility. Remember that you are studying the Book of Romans. Although a speech, magazine article, or some other book may be related, if brought into the conversation it will automatically take time away from the main object of your study, Romans. In the process, the whole group may go off into an interesting-but-time-consuming tangent, thereby making the leader's job more difficult.

While the Bible is consistent within itself and many excellent topical studies build on its consistency, the purpose of *this* study is to examine thoroughly the Book of Romans. Therefore cross referencing (comparing sections of Romans with other portions of Scripture) will cause the same problems as any other tangent. In addition to confusing people who are unfamiliar with other parts of the Bible, cross referencing may cause you to miss Paul's intent in the passage before you.

For example, Paul uses the word "justified" in quite a different way than James. To compare passages using this term does a disservice to both authors.

You'll find each paragraph in Romans is so laden with facts and ideas that you will be thoroughly challenged to straighten these out without turning to other sections of the Scripture.

Naturally, once you have studied a passage as a group, you may refer back to it. Paul assumed his readers had the earlier passage in mind before they read his next section.

7. **Help pace the study.** With the questions and your Bible in front of you, you can be aware of whether or not the study

is progressing at an adequate pace. Each group member shares the responsibility of seeing that the entire passage is covered and the study brought to a profitable close.

8. **Don't criticize another church or religion.** You might find that the quiet person across the table attends just that church—and she won't be back to your group.

9. **Get to know people in your group.** Call each other during the week. Meet socially, share a car pool when convenient, offer to take in a meal if another group member is ill. You may discover that you have more in common than a willingness to study the Bible. Perhaps you'll add to your list of friends.

10. **Invite others to the group.** Any Bible study group grows best as it absorbs new people and new ideas. So share your new-found interest with a friend or neighbor.

11. **Check the material in the back of this book.** You'll find a glossary, a summary of Scripture quotations, and a bibliography. These may help with those questions that still nag at your mind when the day's discussion is over.

12. **Get ready to lead.** It doesn't take a mature Bible student to lead this study. Just asking the questions in this guide should prompt a thorough digging into the passage. In case you feel a little insecure, you'll find a hefty selection of discussion helps in the accompanying Leader's Guide.

So once you've attended the group a few times, sign up to lead a discussion. Remember, the leader learns more than anyone else.

ME, A LEADER?

Sure. Many Bible study groups share the responsibility of leading the discussion. Sooner or later your turn will come. Here are a few pointers to quell any rising panic and help you keep the group working together toward their common goals.

1. **Prepare well ahead of time.** A week or two in advance is not too much. Read the Scripture passage every day for several successive days. Go over the questions in this book, writing out possible answers. Check the *Leader's Manual* for additional ideas, then read the questions again—several times—until the sequence and wording seem natural to you. Don't let yourself be caught during the study with that now-I-wonder-what-comes-next feeling. If some area of the passage still feels fuzzy, check the bibliography on page 127 for extra help. Take careful note of the major area of application. Try living it for a week. By then you will discover some of the difficulties others in your group will face when they try to do

the same. Finally, pray. Ask God to lead you, as you lead the group. Ask Him to make you sensitive to them, to the Scripture, and to Himself. Expect to grow. You will.

2. **Pace the study.** Begin on time. People have come for the purpose of studying the Bible. You don't need to apologize for that. At the appointed hour, simply announce that it is time to begin, open with a prayer, and launch into the study.

Keep an eye on the clock throughout the study. These questions are geared to last for an hour to an hour and fifteen minutes. Don't spend forty-five minutes on the first three questions then have to rush through the rest. On the other hand, if the questions are moving by too quickly, the group is probably not discussing each one thoroughly enough. Slow down. Encourage people to interact with each other's ideas. Be sure they are working through all aspects of the question.

Then end—on time. Many people have other obligations immediately after the study and will appreciate a predictable closing time.

3. **Ask; don't tell.** This study guide is designed for a discussion moderated by a leader. The *Leader's Manual* is *not* a teacher's guide. When you lead the group, your job is like that of a traffic director. You gauge the flow of discussion, being careful that everyone gets a turn. You decide which topics will be treated in what order. You call a halt now and then to send traffic in a new direction. But you do not mount a soapbox and lecture.

Your job is to help each person in the group discover personally the meaning of the passage and to share that discovery with the others. Naturally, since you have prepared the lesson in advance, you will be tempted to tell them all you've learned. Resist this temptation until others have had a chance to discover the same thing. Then, if something is still missing, you may add your own insight to the collection.

4. **Avoid tangents.** The bane of any discussion group is the oh-so-interesting lure of a tangent. These are always time consuming and rarely as profitable as the planned study. A few red flags will warn you that a tangent is about to arise. They are, "My pastor says . . ."; "If we look at Ezekiel (or John, or Revelation) . . ."; "The other day Suzie . . ."

If this occurs, politely listen to the first few sentences. If these confirm your suspicion that a tangent is indeed brewing, thank the person, then direct attention back to the passage.

A leader does, however, need to be sensitive to pressing needs within a group. On rare occasions the tangent grows out of a need much more important than any pre-planned study can meet. In these cases, whisper a quick prayer for guidance, and follow the tangent.

5. **Talk about application.** Each study in this guide leads to a discussion that applies the point of the passage to real life. If you are short of time or if your group feels hesitant in talking about personal things, you'll entertain the thought of omitting these questions. But if you do, your group will lose the main purpose of the study. If God's Word is a book to live by, a few people in your group ought to be willing to talk about how they are going to live in response to it. Putting these intentions into words will strengthen their ability to live out the teachings. The listeners will be challenged to do the same.

So, always allow adequate time to talk over the application questions. Be prepared also to share your own experiences as you have tried to live out the passage.

6. **Try a prayer 'n' share.** Many groups start their session with fifteen minutes of coffee, then hold a short time sharing

personal concerns, needs, and answers to prayer. Afterward, the group members pray briefly for each other, giving thanks and praise, and asking together that God will meet the needs expressed. These short informal sentence prayers are much like casual sharing conversation. The group members simply turn their conversation away from each other and toward God. For many, this brief time of prayer becomes a weekly life line.

7. **Enjoy leading.** It's a big responsibility, but rewarding.

1

WHERE CAN I FIND GOD?

Romans 1

How does God reveal Himself? How can you know about God? Where can you hear His name spoken, read His teachings? Radio, TV, books, magazines, friends, church, teachers, the Bible itself.

Now close your eyes and mentally take all of that away. Place yourself alone in an empty field. The only sound is the twittering of birds. The only sight is green prairie grass and a blue sky laced with fleecy clouds. What would that tell you about God? Could you know God if that were all you had? Alone in that field, think about another question. Would He hold you responsible for knowing Him?

Once you've answered that question, take one further step. Place yourself back in your everyday environment. What does God expect you to know about Himself here? How does He expect you to act on that knowledge?

Read aloud Romans 1:1–17.

1. What can you know about the apostle Paul from these opening paragraphs of his letter? _____

_____

_____

_____

2. What can you know about Paul's readers, the Romans?

_____

_____

3. What can you know about Jesus Christ from these same verses? _____

_____

_____

_____

4. Verses 16 and 17 form the theme around which Paul constructs the rest of his letter. Write five questions that you think a book based on this theme might answer.

_____

_____

_____

_____

Read aloud Romans 1:18–23.

5. What has God made plain, even to those who have never heard of Him? _____

_____

_____

_____

What evidence does He offer them? _____

_____

_____

_____

6. What six steps do those who refuse even this limited information take? _____

_____

_____

_____

_____

_____

_____

_____

7. Why might a person create his own god? _____

_____

_____

_____

_____

8. What people or things are you tempted to put in God's place? _____

_____

_____

_____

Read aloud Romans 1:24–32.
  9. Find three uses of the phrase, "God gave them over. . . ."

In what ways is each "God gave them over" a little worse than the previous one? _____

_____

_____

_____

10. What does this list suggest happens when a person turns away from God, and God lets him have his own way?

_____

_____

11. Survey the list of evils in verses 24–32. Which of these would you categorize as small sins? _____

_____

_____

_____

Which as large ones? _____

_____

_____

_____

Why do you think they are all lumped together here?

_____

_____

12. What does this chapter teach about rejecting the knowledge God gives you about Himself? _____

_____

_____

_____

13. Name one thing God has been teaching you about Himself during the past month. _____

_____

_____

What action, based on this knowledge of God, should you be taking? _____

_____

_____

_____

A Quote To Remember

I am not ashamed of the gospel, because it is the power of God for the salvation of everyone who believes: first for the Jew, then for the Gentile. For in the gospel a righteousness from God is revealed, a righteousness that is by faith from first to last, just as it is written: "The righteous will live by faith."

—*Romans 1:16–17.*

2

DOES ANYONE HAVE A CORNER ON GOD?

Romans 2

A small boy measures his glass of orange juice against his brother's, finds one-half inch difference, and yells, "Mom, it's not fair!"

A seventeen-year-old girl may stay out until midnight on Saturday night while her fourteen-year-old sister must be in at ten o'clock. The younger girl pouts, "It's not fair."

We read in Scripture that God condemns a man who murders his mother just as he does a woman who gossips about her neighbor. So we look skyward and shout, "God, You're not fair!"

Paul ended his first chapter in Romans with an impressive display of the world's sin. He understood how frustrated this could make his readers.

In his defense of the Christian faith, Paul writes the second chapter of Romans in answer to that feeling of resentment about God's justice.

Read aloud Romans 2:1–16.

1. Find as many descriptions as you can of the way God judges a person. _____

   _____

   _____

   _____

   _____

   _____

2. What dangers occur when you judge someone else's sin? (See verses 1–3.) _____

   _____

   _____

   _____

3. A friend tells you, "I only commit small sins; God is kind and will overlook them." According to verses 4–6, how has your friend misunderstood God's kindness? _____

   _____

   _____

   _____

   _____

4. What evidence does Paul offer to support his statement of verse 11 that "God does not show favoritism"? _____

   _____

   _____

   _____

   _____

5. In what ways does God expect different behavior from the person who knows the law and the person who has never heard of God's law? _____

_____

_____

In what ways does God expect the same from each?

_____

_____

6. If you wanted to be called righteous under the system of God's judgment described in verses 1–16, how would you go about it? _____

_____

_____

Read aloud Romans 2:17–29.

7. Why did the Jew think he had a better chance of pleasing God than the Gentile? _____

_____

_____

8. By implication what does Paul accuse these privileged people of doing? _____

_____

_____

9. What great evil resulted when Jews who knew God's laws failed to obey them? _____

_____

_____

10. The one sign that a man was a Jew, one of God's chosen people, was circumcision—an operation performed when he was a baby. What criticism does Paul bring to this standard of identification? _____

_____

_____

11. What false standards do Christians sometimes look for in deciding if they belong in God's family? _____

_____

_____

_____

_____

12. What hope do the last two verses of this chapter offer the person who feels that his own actions will never make him good enough to pass God's judgment? _____

_____

_____

13. What in this chapter makes you thankful that God will allow His Spirit to change the inner you? _____

_____

_____

A Quote To Remember

No, a man is a Jew if he is one inwardly; and circumcision is circumcision of the heart, by the Spirit, not by the written code. Such a man's praise is not from men, but from God.

—Romans 2:29.

3

AM I A SPIRITUAL SNOB?

Romans 3

You've just had the rug pulled out from under you. Raised as a strict Jew, you were taught that your people are "the chosen." You alone were given God's laws, with the awful responsibility of obeying that body of law and, as a result, the awesome privilege of knowing God. Then some fiery-eyed rabbi comes along and declares that anybody can be a Jew. Anybody at all! He accuses you of not keeping God's law and even hints that you couldn't obey it if you tried.

Do you see yourself? Then Romans 3 is addressed to you.

Read again Romans 2:28–29.
 1. Imagine that you are a devout Jew, proud of your faith and culture. How would these words make you feel?

   _____

   What question would you ask Paul? _____

   _____

2. Read in dialogue the questions and answers of Romans 3. Summarize each question and its answer in the chart below.

Verses	Question	Answer
1–2		
3–4		
5–6		
7–8		
9–10		
27a		
27b–28		
29		
31		

Look again at Romans 3:1–9.

3. If you were a Jew ready to turn away from all faith in God, what in these verses might change your mind?

_____

_____

_____

4. What do Paul's answers to these questions teach about the nature of God? _____

_____

_____

_____

Look again at Romans 3:10–18.

5. Find words and phrases here that describe all people.

_____

_____

_____

6. Why would Paul describe in this way a body created by God? _____

_____

_____

_____

7. What kinds of sins might he be speaking of? _____

_____

_____

_____

8. What effect might verses 19–20 have on anyone who hoped that God would receive him because of his good behavior? _____

_____

_____

Read aloud Romans 3:21–31.

9. If the person in the previous question asked you, "Then how can I be received by God?" what would you tell him? (Use the information in verses 21–26.) _____

_____

_____

10. What can you know about God's righteousness from these same verses? _____

_____

_____

11. What reasons does Paul give for not boasting? _____

_____

_____

_____

12. Verse 22 says, "There is no difference." Use the whole chapter to find as many ways as you can in which all people are alike. _____

_____

_____

_____

_____

13. When are you tempted to think you are better than someone else? _____

_____

_____

14. Let's take some time now to confess silently to God the times we have thought and acted as if we were better than someone else.

Time of silent prayer.

A Quote To Remember

Therefore no one will be declared righteous in his sight by observing the law; rather, through the law we become conscious of sin. For all have sinned and fall short of the glory of God.

—*Romans 3:20, 23.*

4

WHAT IS MY CREDIT RATING WITH GOD?

Romans 4

"I'm sorry Ma'am. I can't give you cash for this return."

You sigh and stuff a pair of too-small pants back into a plastic bag and begin to turn away.

"But I can give you a credit slip."

You answer, "I don't want a credit slip. I'd rather have the nineteen dollars and twenty cents."

"But you could buy the whole store," the clerk objects.

"You mean I could buy anything this store sells that's worth nineteen dollars and twenty cents," you correct her.

The sales clerk smiles as if you are a little dense. "No, I mean with this credit slip you can buy the whole store—building, furniture, fixtures, and everything in it."

Fantastic? Yes, but it is something like what God offers those who come to Him.

Paul ended Romans 3 with a question, "Is God the God of the Jews only?" Now he answers the question.

Paul presents the plan in Romans 4.

Read aloud Romans 4.

1. What words and phrases do you find repeated in this chapter? _____

_____

_____

_____

   Based on these phrases, what do you think is the major theme here? _____

_____

_____

Look again at verses 1–8.

2. What is the difference between *wages* and a *gift*? ____

_____

_____

3. If the man referred to by David in verses 7 and 8 received wages, what would his be? _____

_____

Read verses 9–15 again.

4. Of what significance was the timing of Abraham's circumcision? _____

_____

_____

   What difference does this make to modern-day believers?

_____

_____

_____

5. Why would Abraham's promise remain unfulfilled if Abraham was ancestor only to the Jews? _____

_____

_____

_____

Read verses 16–25 again.

6. In what ways did Abraham demonstrate his faith? ____

_____

_____

_____

_____

7. Why were the qualities of God, described in verse 17b, important to Abraham? _____

_____

_____

Why might this kind of power be important to anyone who wants to come to God? _____

_____

_____

8. In what ways does the example of Abraham in chapter 4 prove the point that Paul raised in Romans 3:29–30?

_____

_____

_____

_____

9. Why might this chapter both reassure and disturb Jewish readers? _____

_____

_____

_____

10. According to Romans 4:24–25, what does one need to believe in order to be given credit for righteousness?

_____

_____

_____

11. What do the words "credited as righteousness" imply about the person receiving the credit? _____

_____

_____

12. If you had to choose between going to heaven on the basis of your behavior or on the basis of your faith in the four truths of verses 24–25, which would you choose?

_____

Why? _____

_____

_____

13. God credits you with righteousness the same way He did Abraham, not as wages for your work or even wages for your faith, but as a gift. What difference should this make in the way you feel about yourself? _____

_____

_____

What difference should this make in the way you feel about the work of obeying God? _____

_____

_____

What difference should it make in the way you worship Him? _____

_____

_____

A Quote To Remember

The words "it was credited to him" were written not for him alone, but also for us, to whom God will credit righteousness —for us who believe in him who raised Jesus our Lord from the dead. He was delivered over to death for our sins and was raised to life for our justification.

—*Romans 4:23–25.*

5

HOW CAN I BECOME A CHRISTIAN?

Romans 5

"Are you a Christian?" Ask that question of most people and you'll get a rather uncomfortable sputtering that ends up, "Of course, I'm a Christian." Inside, if not aloud, they'll defend themselves. "I'm not a Buddhist or a Hindu or a Moslem. Of course, I'm a Christian." Or, "I'm a Christian. I go to church every Sunday." Or, "I grew up in a Christian home; I think I was born a Christian." Or, "I think so; I try to be as good as I can."

Confronted with evidence that none of this guarantees Christianity, the unbeliever is apt to respond, "Then why should I become a Christian? I'm doing fine the way I am." In chapter 5 of Romans, Paul begins to answer the why and how of that question.

1. Have someone in your group interview another group member with the following questions. (As you listen, think how you might answer the same question.)

—How did you first see the need of accepting Christ as Savior?

—When and how did you become a Christian?

—What people were specifically influential in bringing you to Christ?

—What did they do that was important in helping you make that decision?

—What passages of Scripture became important to you at that time?

—How are you a different person now than you think you would be if you had not become a Christian?

—What would you like to say to someone who is at the point of deciding whether to give himself to Christ?

Read aloud Romans 4:23–5:5.

2. According to Paul, what characterizes a believer in Jesus Christ? _____

_____

_____

3. Select one of these qualities and tell how it has been helpful to you during the past month. _____

_____

_____

4. How is rejoicing in hope related to rejoicing in suffering?

_____

_____

5. What does the progression of verses 4 and 5 teach about the internal changes in a believer who suffers? _____

_____

_____

6. Why can the believer hope and not be disappointed?

   _____

   How might this power help you to cope when you hope intensely for something but do not receive it? _____

   _____

   _____

   _____

Read aloud Romans 5:6–11.
   7. In what ways does Paul describe our condition before we received Christ's gift? _____

   _____

   8. What words and phrases here convey the possibility of a sinner being made right with God? _____

   _____

   _____

   _____

   9. According to these verses, what are the differences between human love and God's love? _____

   _____

   _____

   _____

Read aloud Romans 5:12–21.
10. What effects did Adam's sin have on all people? _____

   _____

   _____

11. What antidotes does Jesus offer for the destruction brought by Adam's sin? _____

_____

_____

_____

_____

_____

Continue with Question 12 here, or use alternate ending.

12. All people fall under Adam's curse. But only those who receive the gift Jesus offers come into God's family. What information in this chapter would cause you to desire this gift? _____

_____

_____

_____

_____

_____

13. If you desire to receive the gift of eternal life described in verse 21, four steps will lead you to it. Place a check mark next to the steps you have taken.

_____A—Admit I am a sinner.

_____B—Believe Jesus died to forgive that sin.

_____C—Count the cost of committing to Christ all areas of my life from now on.

_____D—Do it. Tell God in prayer that this is what I am doing.

Time of silent prayer.

Alternate ending

12. What in this chapter causes you to want to share the gospel with someone else? _____

_____

_____

13. What information here could you use in presenting the news of Christ's gift? _____

_____

_____

_____

If the opportunity arose, who would you like to speak to this week about their need for salvation? _____

_____

Pray together for each other, asking God to create these opportunities.

A Quote To Remember

Therefore, since we have been justified through faith, we have peace with God through our Lord Jesus Christ, through whom we have gained access by faith into this grace in which we now stand. And we rejoice in the hope of the glory of God. Not only so, but we also rejoice in our sufferings, because we know that suffering produces perseverance; perseverance, character; and character, hope. And hope does not disappoint us, because God has poured out his love into our hearts by the Holy Spirit, whom he has given us.

—Romans 5:1–5.

6

AM I FREE?

Romans 6

"I'm my own boss. I don't punch a clock. Nobody tells me what to do or when to do it. I'm Number One and I take care of me. I'm free."

Sound enviable? But is it possible?

Paul speaks of freedom and slavery in Romans 6. In the end you may well ask, "Am I free? Is anyone?"

Read aloud all of Romans 6.

1. What question does Paul address throughout this sixth chapter? _____

_____

Under what circumstances have you heard or thought this same question? _____

_____

_____

2. Find as many connecting words as you can that link Christ with us. _____

_____

_____

_____

3. In what ways do these verses suggest that a person who becomes a Christian is different than he was before?

_____

_____

_____

4. What do you think is the connection between Christ's death to sin and the Christian's death to sin? _____

_____

_____

_____

5. According to verses 12–14, who are the two masters we must choose between. _____

_____

What do the words "offer" and "instruments" imply about these masters? _____

_____

_____

6. What kind of power does sin have? (See the same verses.)

_____

_____

_____

7. What practical encouragement do these verses offer to help you battle with sin? _____

_____

_____

_____

_____

8. What specific steps could you take in offering your body or any part of it to God? _____

_____

_____

_____

Read again Romans 6:15–23.

9. What evidence does this passage offer for the idea that all people are in some sense slaves? _____

_____

_____

_____

10. What are the results of these two forms of slavery?

_____

_____

_____

_____

_____

_____

11. This passage speaks of slavery to sin. But with many sins, we feel *we* are the boss. We commit them because *we* WANT to. This may be a delusion. What sins do you know of that lead to slavery? _____

_____

_____

_____

12. When has God helped you to resist a sin that you knew would have become your master if you had fallen into it?

_____

_____

_____

13. Pray sentence prayers.
   Thank Jesus for dying to pay for your sins and uniting you to Himself.

   Praise Him for the victory He can give you over sins that trouble you.

   Consider those areas of your life that you would like to keep for yourself, and offer these for Christ's service.

A Quote To Remember

Do not offer the parts of your body to sin, as instruments of wickedness, but rather offer yourselves to God, as those who have been brought from death to life; and offer the parts of your body to him as instruments of righteousness. For sin shall not be your master, because you are not under law, but under grace.

—*Romans 6:13–14*

Take My Life, and Let It Be

Frances R. Havergal

John B. Dykes

1. Take my life, and let it be Con - se - cra - ted, Lord, to thee.
2. Take my hands, and let them move At the im - pulse of thy love.
3. Take my voice, and let me sing, Al - ways, on - ly, for my King.
4. Take my sil — ver and my gold; Not a mite would I with-hold.
5. Take my will, and make it thine; It shall be no long - er mine.
6. Take my love; my Lord, I pour At thy feet its treas-ure - store.

Take my mo-ments and my days; Let them flow in cease-less praise.
Take my feet, and let them be Swift and beau-ti - ful for thee.
Take my lips, and let them be Filled with mes-sag - es from thee.
Take my in - tel-lect, and use Ev - 'ry pow'r as thou shalt choose.
Take my heart, it is thine own; It shall be thy roy - al throne.
Take my-self, and I will be Ev - er, on - ly, all for thee. A - MEN.

7

BUT I CAN'T BE WHAT I SHOULD BE!

Romans 7

"I didn't do it. Honest I didn't." An eight-year-old boy stares at a broken glass and then up at his mother.

A woman helplessly pats her tearful friend on the shoulder. "I'm sorry I said that. I can't imagine what made me do it."

A high school boy's shoulders slump. "You saw me cheat on that algebra test? I didn't plan it that way. I just looked up and there were Sandy's answers spread all over her desk. Right away I knew my problems were wrong and hers were right."

"What a wretched man I am!" shouts the apostle Paul. Is he moaning about a set-back in evangelism? The treachery of a friend? Imprisonment by Roman soldiers? No. These words are wrung from Paul's pen when he looks inside himself and contemplates his own sin.

Can these weak people who lie and hurt and cheat be Christians? Do Christians sin? And what is sin anyway? Paul addresses these questions in Romans 7.

1. Fill in the blanks on this self test.

The situation	What I would do	What I should do
You've just spent all morning cleaning your house. You walk to the corner where your neighborhood mailboxes are all in a row. You are delighted to find your favorite magazine waiting. It seems a fitting reward for your hard work of the morning. While you are looking through your mail a neighbor, Sue, joins you. She has her two-year-old Timmy in tow. You notice that Sue looks tired and you say so. She answers, "Yes, the baby had me up all night with an ear infection. Finally she's asleep but Timmy picked today to utterly refuse a nap. I'm beat." You . . .		
Your husband has been really crabby lately. It seems as if he's almost looking for things to be angry about. Today he walks in from work and demands, "Did you feed the cat?" Actually you've been gone all day and just got home yourself. And you *did* forget the cat. You say . . .		
You are standing in line at the grocery checkout. Money has been tight lately and you've added up every item in your cart to be sure you don't spend over your limit. Lying on the floor in front of you is a ten-dollar bill. You . . .		

You're running late for an appointment. You have your three small children bundled in snowsuits and you're attempting to hussle them out the door. The youngest says, "I have to go potty." You . . .		
Peggy is new in your neighborhood. She's from Germany and doesn't seem to like America much. She's opinionated and a non-stop talker. She has a reputation for stopping in to have morning coffee and hanging around for evening dinner. She's angry, lonely, and has lots of problems inside. Nobody seems to like her much. You glance out your kitchen window at 9:00 A.M. and Peggy's pecking on your door. You . . .		
You are at an afternoon coffee klatsch. The object of discussion is a rather oddball person who is not present. The group has had several good laughs over her already. But no one has mentioned yet that she once went chasing after the garbage truck in her nightgown. Maybe you're the only one who knows it. You . . .		

Do your two columns look exactly alike? Or did you find a few differences in what you *should* do and what you *would* do? The apostle Paul didn't always do what he knew he should either. Let's see what he wrote about it.

Read aloud Romans 7.

2. Describe the kind of Christian who needs to hear the way Paul speaks of sin in this chapter. _____

   _____

   _____

   _____

   _____

3. How is this different from the kind of person who needed to hear chapter 6? _____

   _____

   _____

   _____

Look again at verses 1–6.

4. In what way is the law like a husband? _____

   _____

   _____

5. How is our relationship to the law changed when we become a Christian? _____

   _____

   _____

   _____

Read again verses 7–13.

6. List the specific things Paul says about sin and the law in these verses. _____

   _____

   _____

_____

_____

_____

_____

_____

_____

7. What is the relationship between sin and the law? _____

_____

_____

_____

8. Under what circumstances might a law make you more likely to sin? _____

_____

_____

9. What discovery did the law help Paul to make about himself? (See verse 13.) _____

_____

_____

Read again verses 12–24.

10. What conflict was going on inside Paul? _____

_____

_____

What progress did each side make? _____

_____

_____

What was the result of the battle? _____

_____

_____

11. Under what circumstances have you experienced this same kind of conflict? _____

_____

_____

_____

_____

12. What is the difference between offering yourself to sin, as in Romans 6:13, and the "slavery to sin" that Romans 7:14–25 describes? _____

_____

_____

_____

_____

13. Count the number of "I's" in verses 14–23. _____

What significance does this give to verse 24? _____

_____

_____

_____

Why is it meaningful that Paul says "who" and not "how" in verse 24? _____

_____

_____

_____

Read aloud Romans 7:25 – 8:1.

14. What hope can we have in the battle with sin? _____

_____

_____

_____

_____

15. Sometimes we can be more successful in fighting sin if we determine in advance what our temptations are likely to be. What do you think will be your greatest area of struggle with sin in the coming week? _____

_____

_____

_____

Pray together for each other about these battles.

16. Sing the hymn on the next page as praise to Jesus and encouragement to one another.

A Quote To Remember

For in my inner being I delight in God's law; but I see another law at work in the members of my body, waging war against the law of my mind and making me a prisoner of the law of sin at work within my members. What a wretched man I am! Who will rescue me from this body of death? Thanks be to God—through Jesus Christ our Lord!

—*Romans 7:22–25.*

Praise the Savior, Ye Who Know Him

Thomas Kelly

Traditional German Melody

1. Praise the Sav - ior, ye who know Him! Who can tell how much we owe Him?
2. Je - sus is the name that charms us; He for con - flict fits and arms us;
3. Trust in Him, ye saints, for - e - ver; He is faith - ful, chang - ing ne - ver;
4. Keep us, Lord, O keep us cleav - ing To Thy - self and still be - liev - ing,
5. Then we shall be where we would be, Then we shall be what we should be;

Glad - ly let us ren - der to Him All we are and have.
No - thing moves and no - thing harms us While we trust in Him.
Nei - ther force nor guile can se - ver Those He loves from Him.
Till the hour of our re - ceiv - ing Pro - mised joys with Thee.
Things that are not now, nor could be, Soon shall be our own. A - men.

8

HOW CAN I KNOW THE HOLY SPIRIT?

Romans 8:1–17

God, the Father—we think of our own dad, someone who is warm, fair, loving.

God, the Son—we think of Jesus, a man who made sick people well, taught ordinary men, and loved children.

God, the Holy Spirit—we can't see Him or touch Him. He is not like anyone we know. His name suggests that He may be unpredictable, mysterious, intangible, something like a ghost. Yet Paul says in Romans that the Holy Spirit lives inside the believer. Understandably that may make us feel uneasy.

Romans 8 is sometimes called a hymn to the Holy Spirit. We should know Him better by the close of our study; perhaps we'll fear Him less.

Read aloud Romans 8:1–4.
1. What solution does God offer to the person who cannot keep from sinning? _____

_____

2. What part does each member of the Trinity play in this solution? _____

_____

_____

_____

Scan the entire passage of Romans 8:1–17.

3. What names does Paul give to the Holy Spirit? _____

_____

_____

_____

What do these names tell us about the character of the Holy Spirit? _____

_____

_____

_____

_____

Read aloud Romans 8:5–9.

4. What happens when we set our minds on what nature desires? _____

_____

_____

How is this different from the effects of setting our minds on the Spirit? _____

_____

_____

5. What evidence do you find here that you can't have a little sin and a little of the Holy Spirit, without being wholly committed to either one or the other? _____

_____

_____

_____

_____

_____

6. What information in verses 5–9 would make you want to submit to the Spirit's control? _____

_____

_____

_____

_____

Why might you hesitate? _____

_____

_____

_____

_____

Read aloud Romans 8:9–11.
7. According to these verses, what is dead and what is alive? _____

_____

_____

_____

8. What do you think Paul means when he says, "Your body is dead" (verse 10) but "the Spirit . . . will also give life to your mortal bodies" (verse 11)? _____

_____

_____

_____

_____

_____

9. What evidence does Paul offer that the Holy Spirit is able to give this kind of life? _____

_____

_____

Read aloud Romans 8:12–17.

10. In what ways are a son and a slave alike? _____

_____

_____

How do they differ? _____

_____

_____

11. In what ways does becoming a child of God free you from being a "slave to fear"? _____

_____

_____

_____

_____

What particular fears are you now learning to turn over to God? _____

_____

_____

12. How does the Christian differ from the unbeliever in his relation to God the Father? _____

_____

_____

To the Son? _____

_____

To the Holy Spirit? _____

_____

13. Find each place where the Holy Spirit is mentioned. What does each reference say about the work of the Holy Spirit? (Review all of Romans 8:1–17. Add also verses 26–27.) _____

_____

_____

_____

_____

From these observations, summarize in about two sentences the relationship between the believer and the Holy Spirit. _____

_____

_____

_____

14. What do you appreciate about the Holy Spirit? _____

_____

_____

_____

In what ways are you uneasy about Him? _____

_____

_____

_____

What changes do you think would occur in your life if you allowed the Holy Spirit to have more control? ____

_____

_____

_____

15. Write a prayer to God, the Holy Spirit, expressing some of these thoughts. _____

_____

_____

_____

_____

_____

_____

_____

If you choose to, read your prayer aloud as a closing to your time of Bible study.

A Quote To Remember

The Spirit himself testifies with our spirit that we are God's children. Now if we are children, then we are heirs—heirs of God and co-heirs with Christ, if indeed we share in his sufferings in order that we may also share in his glory.

—*Romans 8:16–17.*

9

HOW CAN I PRAISE GOD?

Romans 8:18–39

What do you mean when you say, "I love you"? Do you say it often? To whom? A lot of people or a special few? How do you feel when someone directs those three special words to you?

"Smile, God loves you," is not just an empty slogan on a lapel button. God really does love us; He says so in a hundred ways. Romans 8 describes a few of these.

But do we love God in return? To love God, first we must know Him—who He is and what He does. Here too, Romans 8 reveals God. It's as though a heavy curtain is parted for a moment and we get just a glimpse of God Almighty, Maker of Heaven and Earth.

How can we respond? We can take the time to know Him, to learn His character, His qualities. Once we've done that, the only natural response is worship—an expression of our love for Him.

Read aloud Romans 8:18–39.

1. Find one sentence or thought that you particularly enjoy in this passage. _____

   _____

   _____

   Why is it special to you? _____

   _____

   _____

Read again verses 18–25.

2. What hints of unfinishedness do you find here? _____

   _____

   _____

   _____

   _____

3. What changes do you think will occur when God finishes His work in us and the rest of His creation? _____

   _____

   _____

4. What words here show the intensity of the desire for this change? _____

   _____

   _____

   _____

   _____

5. What is the believer waiting for? _____

_____

_____

What does this imply about what God has not yet done in the believer? _____

_____

_____

6. How would you define "hope" from what Paul says here about its quality? _____

_____

_____

Why does this kind of hope make it possible for you to wait patiently for these changes in you and in the rest of God's creation? _____

_____

_____

Read again verses 26–27.

7. In what ways does the Holy Spirit form a link between God the Father and the believer? _____

_____

_____

_____

8. On what occasions have you been thankful that the Holy Spirit works the way these verses describe? _____

_____

_____

9. How might this knowledge about the Holy Spirit affect
your praying? _____

_____

_____

Read verses 28–30.

10. What conditions does Paul attach to the statement, "In
all things God works for the good"? _____

_____

_____

_____

_____

11. Under what circumstances have you found it hard to
believe such a promise? _____

_____

_____

_____

When might this promise be a comfort to you? _____

_____

_____

_____

12. What does verse 28 imply about the nature of God?

_____

_____

_____

13. What reasons does Paul give for God making such a statement about Himself? _____

_____

_____

_____

_____

14. List the progression of five steps that begins with "God foreknew." _____

_____

_____

_____

15. Look up the definition for each of these five terms. (See Glossary on page 119.) Restate the progression, assuming that your listener has no knowledge of theological language. _____

_____

_____

_____

_____

_____

Read again Romans 8:31–39.

16. Read each of the five rhetorical questions in verses 32–35 aloud. Then give the answer Paul seems to be asking for. _____

_____

_____

17. What part does Jesus Christ play in this security that God offers? _____

_____

_____

18. What phrases here show the extent to which God binds the believer to the love of Christ? _____

_____

_____

_____

19. What information from these verses makes you feel that you could be the conqueror of verse 37? _____

_____

_____

20. Find one sentence in Romans 8 that demonstrates a quality of God that you appreciate. _____

_____

_____

_____

Pray, praising God for that quality.

A Quote To Remember

For I am convinced that neither death nor life, neither angels nor demons, neither the present nor the future, nor any powers, neither height nor depth, nor anything else in all creation, will be able to separate us from the love of God that is in Christ Jesus our Lord.

—*Romans 8:38–39.*

10

IS ANYONE IN CHARGE UP THERE?

Romans 9

Is anyone in charge up there? Do nations rise and fall at the whim of kings? Or is Someone lording it over the kings?

What about me? Do I decide the course of my life? When I chose to follow Jesus Christ rather than to "grab all the gusto" this one time around, was that my decision alone? Or was some Higher Power drawing me first to Himself and bringing order to a tangled life?

And is the universe a tangle anyway? Or is there some pattern perceived only by a Master Weaver?

In Romans 9, Paul asks these questions, then he reaches some challenging conclusions. Try them.

Read aloud Romans 9:1–5.

1. What change do you see in Paul's mood as he shifts from chapter 8 to chapter 9? _____

_____

What reasons can you suggest for this change? _____

_____

_____

_____

2. What words and phrases show Paul's love for the Jews?

_____

_____

_____

3. What blessings had God already given the Jews? _____

_____

_____

_____

_____

Read aloud Romans 9:6–14.

4. What arguments does Paul use to weaken the Jews' claim that they are chosen by God through their biological ancestry? _____

_____

_____

_____

5. If you were among the Jews reading this letter, why might you ask, "Is God unjust?" _____

_____

_____

_____

Read aloud Romans 9:14–21.

6. In what ways were Esau and Pharaoh alike? _____

_____

_____

_____

7. If we assume, as Romans 1–3 teaches, that everyone deserves the wrath God extended to Esau, what effect does this have on your reaction to God's selecting a chosen people? _____

_____

_____

_____

8. What does the illustration of the potter and the clay tell about the way people and God relate to each other?

_____

_____

_____

9. What accusation against God is implied by verse 19?

_____

_____

_____

What has Paul said thus far about God's character that replies to that accusation? _____

_____

_____

_____

Read aloud Romans 9:22–29.

10. Review the four quotes from the prophets (verses 25–29). How is each one a defense for Paul's statement that God calls "not only from the Jews but also from the Gentiles"?

_____

_____

_____

_____

_____

_____

_____

_____

Read aloud Romans 9:30–33.

11. The last paragraph switches from God's perspective of salvation to man's. What reasons visible to humans does Paul give for many Jews not attaining righteousness?

_____

_____

12. Why do you think God used the term "stumbling stone" to describe Jesus? _____

_____

_____

13. Describe in one sentence the characteristic of God revealed in this chapter. _____

_____

_____

14. Of what value would this chapter be to a church composed of a mixture of Jewish and Gentile Christians?

_____

_____

_____

_____

15. You can't possibly know whether God has chosen you to be part of His family until after you have made a decision to commit your life to Jesus Christ, accepting His offer of salvation. After that decision, what comfort might you find in discovering that God had already chosen you?

_____

_____

_____

_____

Sing together the song "I Sought the Lord" (printed on next page).

A Quote To Remember

For he says to Moses,
"I will have mercy on whom I have mercy, and I will have compassion on whom I have compassion."

—*Romans 9:15.*

I Sought the Lord

"The Pilgrim Hymnal"

George W. Chadwick

1. I sought the Lord, and af - ter - ward I knew He moved my soul to seek Him, seek - ing me; It was not I that found, O Sa - vior true; No, I was found of Thee.

2. Thou didst reach forth Thy hand and mine en - fold; I walked and sank not on the storm-vexed sea; 'Twas not so much that I on Thee took hold, As Thou, dear Lord, on me.

3. I find, I walk, I love; but O the whole Of love is but my an - swer, Lord, to Thee! For Thou were long be - fore-hand with my soul; Al - ways Thou lov - edst me. A - men.

11

HOW CAN I SHARE MY FAITH?

Romans 10

Leaflets flutter from an airplane filling the sewers with "Jesus Saves."

Bumper stickers blare "Honk if you love Jesus."

A man paces up and down the street wearing placards of doom: "The end is near; prepare to meet your God."

A pastor thunders vivid images of hell from the pulpit until every nine-year-old in the audience either cringes under his seat or comes running down the aisle.

Evangelism? Doubtful.

Yet even if we are turned off by such methods, we aren't quite off the hook—for God does give every Christian the responsibility to spread the gospel.

To figure out your share of that job, ask yourself three questions as you study Romans 10. 1) What is the purpose of witnessing? 2) What must a person do to become a Christian? 3) What can I do to help one person take those steps?

1. Before reading the chapter in Romans, mark each question true or false.

True	False	
_____	_____	**a.** Since God chooses who will be saved, Christians are freed from the responsibility to witness.
_____	_____	**b.** The main purpose in witnessing is to give the message of salvation; the rest is up to God.
_____	_____	**c.** The minimum requirement for salvation is to accept Jesus as personal Savior. Anything more than that simply makes someone who was already a Christian a better Christian.
_____	_____	**d.** It is possible to be a "secret Christian" by believing in Jesus but never telling anyone about it.
_____	_____	**e.** It is almost impossible for the Jews to be saved; they have had their chance already so God no longer cares about them.

Read aloud Romans 10:1–13.
2. How did the Jews' method of seeking righteousness work at cross purposes with Paul's desire for them? (See verses 1–4.) _____

_____

_____

_____

_____

_____

_____

3. What is the difference between the righteousness that is by law and the righteousness that is by faith? _____

_____

_____

_____

_____

4. What part does the heart and mouth play in this righteousness by faith? ___ _____

_____

_____

What must you believe; what must you confess? _____

_____

_____

What is God's part in this procedure? _____

_____

_____

5. What does it mean to have a "lord"? _____

_____

_____

_____

_____

What changes would take place in a person who says, "Jesus is my Lord," and means it? _____

_____

_____

_____

_____

6. Why do you think that believing in your heart is not enough, according to this passage? _____

_____

_____

_____

7. If someone asked you, "How can I become a Christian?" what would you say? _____

_____

_____

_____

8. What assurance could you give such a person that God would accept him if he took these steps? _____

_____

_____

_____

_____

Read aloud Romans 10:14–21.

9. Trace the sequence in verses 13–15: What has to happen first, then second, third, and so on, in the chain of events?

_____

_____

_____

10. Why might a person hear the gospel but not be able to understand it? _____

_____

_____

Why might he understand it but not accept it? _____

_____

_____

What could you do to help such a person? _____

_____

_____

_____

What could you not do? _____

_____

11. Review Paul's last four quotations from the Old Testament. In what ways does God show His love for the Jews?

_____

_____

_____

_____

12. What is hard about witnessing? _____

_____

_____

_____

When have you shared the gospel but later wished you had done it differently? Tell about it. _____

_____

_____

_____

13. What is the primary purpose of telling someone about Jesus? (See verses 1 and 13.) _____

_____

_____

14. What other reasons do people sometimes have for sharing the gospel? _____

_____

_____

_____

How might some of these actually keep a person from becoming a Christian? _____

_____

_____

_____

_____

15. Write the name of one person you would like to bring to Christ. _____

What is the best thing you can do to bring this about?

_____

_____

When and how do you hope to begin? _____

_____

_____

_____

A Quote To Remember

That if you confess with your mouth, "Jesus is Lord," and believe in your heart that God raised him from the dead, you will be saved. For it is with your heart that you believe and are justified, and it is with your mouth that you confess and are saved.

—*Romans 10:9–10.*

12

DOES HISTORY MAKE A DIFFERENCE?

Romans 11

Roots. Biologists tell us a tree's roots are as wide-reaching as its branches. Some people trace the roots of their family tree back hundreds of years, spotting a preacher here and a drunkard there and sometimes a hint of royalty. With each new discovery in the root system they look inside themselves hoping (or fearing) to find the same qualities. Our roots can give us confidence in the gifts we have inherited while at the same time posting warnings about pitfalls.

Spiritual roots give us the same kind of perspective. So, in Romans 11, Paul traces the roots of the Christian faith. But he doesn't stop with Jesus. Like the roots of a huge old tree, our roots reach way back in history—to Abraham.

Read aloud Romans 11:1–10

1. What examples does Paul cite to answer the question, "Did God reject His people?" _____

_____

_____

_____

_____

In each case, how did the Jews escape being rejected?

_____

_____

2. What picture do you form of God from verses 7–10?

_____

_____

_____

How does Romans 10:2–3 soften this picture? _____

_____

_____

Why is attempting to win salvation by our own right-eousness a direct insult to God? _____

_____

_____

_____

Read aloud Romans 11:11–24.
3. What evidence does Paul offer to show that the Jews have not stumbled beyond recovery? _____

_____

_____

_____

_____

4. Draw a picture of the ingrafted tree and the chopped-off branches. Label the parts.

In what ways do both the tree and the grafted-in branch benefit from the operation? (Use verses 18–24 and your drawing.) _____

_____

_____

_____

5. In what sense is the Christian faith also Jewish? _____

_____

_____

_____

_____

In what ways is it distinctively Christian? _____

_____

_____

_____

_____

6. What warnings does Paul offer any Christian who feels smug about being chosen by God? _____

_____

_____

_____

_____

7. Why is God's grafting in of Gentiles an offer of hope to the Jews? _____

_____

_____

Read aloud Romans 11:25–36.

8. According to these verses, what would you say is in the future of Israel? _____

_____

_____

9. What evidence has Paul presented in chapter 11 to answer his opening question, "Did God reject his people?" and thereby prove his statement of verse 29? _____

_____

_____

_____

_____

In what ways is chapter 11 an extension of Romans 8:29–30 and 38–39? _____

_____

_____

_____

10. What connections do you see behind man's disobedience and God's mercy? (See Romans 11:30–32.) _____

_____

_____

_____

11. In what different ways does Paul describe God's greatness in his hymn of praise in verses 33–36? _____

_____

_____

_____

_____

12. What difference does it make to you that, while Christianity began two thousand years ago, its roots go even further back, to Abraham? _____

_____

_____

_____

What do you appreciate more about the Christian faith because of these roots? _____

_____

_____

How might you worship God better because of this knowledge? _____

_____

_____

_____

A Quote To Remember

Oh, the depth of the riches of the wisdom
   and knowledge of God!
How unsearchable his judgments,
   and his paths beyond tracing out!
"Who has known the mind of the Lord?
Or who has been his counselor?"
"Who has ever given to God,
   that God should repay him?"
For from him and through him and to him are all things.
To him be the glory forever! Amen.

—*Romans 11:33–36.*

The Jews

Poor nation, whose sweet sap and juice
   Our scions have purloined and left you dry:
Whose streams we got by the apostles' sluice,
   And use in baptism, while ye pine and die:
Who by not keeping once, became a debtor,
   And now by keeping lose the letter—

Oh that my prayers! mine, alas!
   Oh that some Angel might a trumpet sound,
At which the Church, falling upon her face,
   Should cry so loud until the trump were drowned,
And by that cry, of her dear Lord obtain
   That your sweet sap might come again!

                                 —*George Herbert*

13

SHOULD I GIVE AWAY MYSELF?

Romans 12

What is the one possession you value most? Your house? Your car? Your dog or horse? How about your china cabinet or the photo albums you started when you were nine?

Whatever this most favored possession is, how does it compare with the way you value your body—the inner you which that body houses? Likely you could give away everything else, but still hang onto that one most valued possession—yourself.

Yet, God asks for exactly that one most valued of all gifts: your body. He talks about a "living sacrifice."

Read aloud Romans 12:1–2.
1. What does Paul consider an appropriate response to the God he has described thus far in Romans? (Don't forget verse 2.) _____

_____

2. What is the difference between a Christian living sacrifice and a Jewish burnt offering? _____

_____

_____

_____

3. What do you think would be difficult about offering yourself as a living sacrifice? _____

_____

_____

_____

4. What can you gain from offering yourself in this way?

_____

_____

_____

Read aloud Romans 12:3–8.

5. In what ways does a sacrifice of our bodies to God also become a sacrifice to other believers? _____

_____

_____

_____

_____

6. What spiritual gifts are listed here? _____

_____

_____

_____

What instructions does Paul give for the use of each?

_____

_____

_____

_____

What would happen if each of these gifts were used in a selfish way? _____

_____

_____

_____

_____

7. Look at yourself with the sober judgment described in verse 3. What gifts or abilities do you see in yourself? (Don't limit yourself to the 7 listed in the passage.)

_____

_____

_____

_____

What steps can you take to develop one or more of those gifts? _____

_____

_____

_____

How might a deep belief that "each member belongs to all the others" affect the way you use your gift? _____

_____

_____

_____

Read aloud Romans 12:9–21.

8. What do the action words of these verses tell you about the nature of "sincere love"? _____

_____

_____

_____

9. What difficulties does Paul foresee for the Christian who sacrifices himself? _____

_____

_____

_____

10. When have you hesitated to associate with someone of lower position than you (someone too young or too old, less talented, less wealthy, less attractive)? _____

_____

_____

_____

What does this hesitation tell you about the way you value yourself and that other person? _____

_____

_____

11. How is the Christian to deal with someone who opposes him? _____

_____

_____

_____

What would you find difficult about treating an enemy this way? _____

_____

_____

_____

What hints do you find in the passage that say you will not always be able to find a peaceful solution? _____

_____

_____

12. What have you learned in Romans that might give you courage to repay evil with good? _____

_____

_____

_____

_____

Note: "You will heap burning coals on his head"—*The New Bible Commentary* interprets this graphic phrase to mean "Give him a burning sense of shame" (p. 1041).

13. Think of one person with whom you are experiencing friction. _____

_____

Without naming the person aloud, what first step can you take to obey the commands of this chapter? _____

_____

_____

_____

_____

A Quote To Remember

Therefore, I urge you, brothers, in view of God's mercy, to offer your bodies as living sacrifices, holy and pleasing to God—which is your spiritual worship. Do not conform any longer to the pattern of this world, but be transformed by the renewing of your mind. Then you will be able to test and approve what God's will is—his good, pleasing and perfect will.

—Romans 12:1–2.

14

HOW MUCH DO I OWE?

Romans 13

Rate yourself on a scale of 1 to 6 by circling the number. (1—always true; 2—usually true; 3—sometimes true; 4—sometimes false; 5—usually false; 6—always false.)

a. I don't feel bound by picky laws like speed limits and "don't walk" signs.   1 2 3 4 5 6

b. Just let my husband "command" me to do something and I balk. If he wants it done, he'd better ask nicely.   1 2 3 4 5 6

c. If the boss isn't looking, I take a break. I get out of as much work as I can.   1 2 3 4 5 6

d. I don't ask the advice and instruction of elders in my church.   1 2 3 4 5 6

e. I speak my mind about government officials; if they want my respect they'll have to earn it.   1 2 3 4 5 6

f. I obey God's laws—but only those that seem practical for my situation.   1 2 3 4 5 6

1. Mention all the people you can think of who have authority over you. _____

   _____

   _____

   Why is submission to authority unpleasant? _____

   _____

   _____

   _____

Read aloud Romans 13:1–8.
2. What reasons does Paul give for submitting to authority?

   _____

   _____

   _____

3. Why do you think that God established structures of authority within the nation? _____

   _____

   _____

   Within the church? _____

   _____

   Within the home? _____

   _____

4. In what different capacities do authorities act as God's servants in this passage? _____

   _____

   _____

5. What advantage is it to you that those who have authority are established by God? _____

_____

_____

_____

6. Do you think you should submit to an authority who does not himself submit to God? _____

Why, or why not? _____

_____

_____

At what point would you feel justified in not submitting to such an authority? (See also Matthew 22:21 and Acts 5:29.) _____

_____

_____

_____

Read aloud Romans 13:8–14.

7. What advice does Paul give to the Christian about managing his business affairs? _____

_____

_____

_____

8. If you were to obey this command, what effect would it have on your credit practices? _____

_____

_____

Your work? _____

_____

The way you treat your parents or in-laws? _____

_____

_____

The way you speak of your country's president? _____

_____

_____

9. How does God's love for us make the debt of love different from other debts? _____

_____

_____

_____

10. List some ways you show love and care for yourself.

_____

_____

What changes would take place if you began to treat others with that same concern? _____

_____

_____

_____

11. What reasons for urgency does Paul point out? _____

_____

_____

_____

Note: "Salvation" in verse 11 refers to the redemption of the body when it is either raised from the dead or caught up at Christ's return to meet him in the air. (*The Epistle of Paul to the Romans,* by F. F. Bruce, p. 242.)

12. If you were quite convinced that Christ would return at any moment, what change would you make first in your behavior? _____

   _____

   _____

   _____

   _____

13. Look again at your self-test on page 101. In what setting do you have the most trouble dealing with authority?

   _____

   What steps could you take to bring your behavior more in line with the teachings of this chapter? _____

   _____

   _____

   _____

   _____

A Quote To Remember

Everyone must submit himself to the governing authorities, for there is no authority except that which God has established. The authorities that exist have been established by God. Consequently, he who rebels against the authority is rebelling against what God has instituted, and those who do so will bring judgment on themselves.

—*Romans 13:1–2.*

15

SHOULD MY NEIGHBOR'S CONSCIENCE BE MY GUIDE?

Romans 14:1–15:13

Christians have made a few strange rules for each other. For example at some time or place:

—You could wear buttons on your coat, but not a zipper.

—You could sleep on Sunday afternoon but not knit.

—You could drink root beer but not Coke.

—You could eat until you were fifty pounds overweight, but not smoke a cigarette.

—You could go to a doctor if you had a cold but not if you were giving birth to a baby.

How should a mature Christian respond to such strange rules—rules based on someone else's conscience? Romans brings up a few such rules from the first century. Then Paul tells his readers how to cope with them.

Read aloud Romans 14:1–8.

1. What differences between Christians does Paul cite?

_____

_____

_____

_____

2. What attitudes and actions does Paul say will help these people get along together? _____

_____

_____

_____

_____

_____

_____

3. According to Paul, who is a "weaker brother"? How is he defined here? _____

_____

_____

_____

4. Why would a person "fully convinced in his own mind" (verse 5) be able to tolerate a person who disagrees with him? _____

_____

_____

_____

_____

Read aloud Romans 14:9–23.

5. Why did Christ's death and return to life make it wrong for us to judge each other over disputable matters?

_____

_____

_____

_____

6. What guidelines does Paul propose for knowing when you should limit your own freedom because of another Christian? _____

_____

_____

_____

_____

7. Unclean and clean food (food prepared according to Jewish ceremonial law) was a big issue to early Christians. It represented a lot of work for those who kept the law and a big freedom to those who didn't. Yet Paul says to those who enjoyed that freedom, "Do not destroy the work of God for the sake of food" (verse 20). What did he mean for them to do? _____

_____

_____

_____

8. Rewrite that sentence, completing it with several phrases that represent a controversy among Christians you know. (Be sure not to include anything expressly forbidden by God.)

Do not destroy the work of God for the sake of:

_____

_____

_____

_____

Do you need to limit your own freedom on any of these instances? _____

If so, to what extent? _____

_____

9. Are you being a "weaker brother" and thereby inconveniencing other Christians over minor issues? _____

_____

If so, how might you change? _____

_____

How does verse 23 limit this change? _____

_____

_____

_____

10. Why do you think that where right and wrong is in question, Paul's emphasis is on the free person giving in to the person with scruples? _____

_____

_____

_____

Read aloud Romans 15:1–13.

11. In what ways does Christ bring about unity among His people? _____

    _____

    _____

    _____

12. Early Jewish Christians found it hard to accept Gentiles into their church. (Gentiles felt free from Jewish ceremonial laws, yet Jewish Christians continued to obey them.) What does Paul say in verses 8–13 that might make it easier for Jews to accept these Gentiles? _____

    _____

    _____

    _____

    If early Gentile Christians obeyed Paul's instructions in these two chapters, how might their behavior have changed in a way easier for Jews to accept? _____

    _____

    _____

    _____

13. What sources of hope does Paul offer that these differences really can be resolved? _____

    _____

    _____

    _____

    _____

    _____

14. If your church were to follow the teachings of these chapters, what changes would you see? _____

_____

_____

_____

_____

How could you begin to bring about one of these changes? _____

_____

_____

A Quote To Remember

Do not destroy the work of God for the sake of food. All food is clean, but it is wrong for a man to eat anything that causes someone else to stumble. It is better not to eat meat or drink wine or to do anything else that will cause your brother to fall.

—*Romans 14:20–21.*

16

WHAT MAKES LIFE WORTH LIVING?

Romans 15:14 –16:27

"Ring-ng-ng."

It's 3:00 A.M. and the hot line crisis phone sounds off. A strangled voice says, "I've got a bottle of pills in my hand and I'm going to end it all. Nothing in my life is worthwhile." Every night it happens somewhere in this country.

What brings a person to such a decision? Perhaps it's a lack of friends, a lost job, a broken love, a vanished faith—a sense that everything he does is futile; that he is a worthless person.

More important—how can we keep from becoming that voice on the phone? Paul closes his letter to the Romans with some personal notes. He gives greetings to people he knew in Rome, brief sketches of friends with him in Corinth, and thoughts about himself and his work. In these comments he reveals himself and his own purpose in life. Through what Paul says we can discover what made his life worthwhile— and perhaps get help for our own.

Read aloud Romans 15:14–22.

1. What words and phrases reflect the way Paul feels about his work? _____

_____

_____

_____

2. What does Paul see as valuable in his work? _____

_____

_____

_____

Read aloud Romans 15:23–33.

3. Detail Paul's plans for the future. _____

_____

_____

How does he feel about these plans? _____

_____

_____

4. In what ways does Paul help his readers to pray intelligently for him? _____

_____

_____

_____

_____

_____

Silently read Romans 16:1–16.

5. What evidence is there that Paul's relationships with people were satisfying? _____

_____

_____

_____

6. What characteristics in a friend were important to Paul?

_____

_____

7. How might this listing help you make wise selections in your own friendships? _____

_____

_____

_____

Read aloud Romans 16:17–27.

8. What is the difference between the "disputable matters" of 14:1 and the "divisions" of 16:17? _____

_____

_____

_____

_____

9. In what ways do the works of God mentioned in verses 25–27 relate to the letter Paul has just completed?

_____

_____

_____

10. What ingredients seem to make Paul's life worthwhile?

_____

_____

_____

_____

11. If you hope to structure your life so that you find satisfaction in each of several areas, what groundwork should you be laying now?

Consider:

Work—If you viewed all of your work as some form of service to God, what would you begin to do? _____

_____

_____

_____

_____

Family—Since you will always "live with" your family, either in person or in memory, what should you begin to do now? _____

_____

_____

_____

Friendships—If you loved your best friend as much as you love yourself, what would you begin to do? _____

_____

_____

_____

Worship—If you believed that your relationship with God was more important than any other relationship in your life, what would you begin to do? _____

_____

_____

_____

_____

A Quote To Remember

Therefore I glory in Christ Jesus in my service to God.

—*Romans 15:17.*

GLOSSARY

Note: Glossary entries are based on phrasing of the *New International Version* of the Bible and reflect meanings implied in the context of Paul's letter to the Romans.

atonement—the reconciliation of man to God through the death of Jesus Christ

call—a summons from God to bear the name of Christian and to belong to God in Christ

circumcision—a minor operation in which loose skin at the tip of the penis is removed, a Jewish rite performed as a sign of inclusion in the covenant between God and Abraham (Gen. 17:9–14)

conform—to become similar or identical with; to fit a mold

credit—to add something to a person's account, to number it among his belongings; to impute

elect—those people chosen by God through the process of election

election—1) the act of choice whereby God picks an individual or group out of a larger company for a purpose or destiny of his own appointment; 2) the act by which God chooses individual sinners for eternal life through divine mercy

faith—the attitude by which a person abandons all reliance on his own efforts to obtain salvation; instead he has complete trust in Christ alone to give salvation as a gift

foreknow—to have previous knowledge of, to know beforehand; also possibly to have planned in advance

Gentile—a person of a non-Jewish nation or faith

glorify—the ultimate state of being completely conformed to the image of Jesus Christ

grace—the attitude by which God treats a person, though guilty, as if there had been no sin

holiness—the character quality of growing to be like Christ and of being one who is set apart for him

inner being—the Christian's true self as seen by God and known, partially, in his own conscience

justification—God's forgiveness and treatment of sinners as if they had never sinned by crediting them with Christ's sinlessness

justified—the legal state before God of a person who has received justification

the law—the revelation of the will of God set forth in the Old Testament

neighbor—anyone with whom I come into contact

predestined—literally, determined in advance; in the Bible, this refers to God's determining in advance a way of saving us; many believe it also refers to God's deliberate election of certain individuals for salvation

reconciliation—the doing away of enmity; the act of bringing together two formerly hostile parties, thus making peace between them; in salvation this is a gift from Christ

redemption—deliverance from some evil state by payment of a price

righteous—1) perfectly obedient to the law, mind, and will of God; 2) "declared right" with God because of Christ's death

righteousness—perfect conformity to the law, mind, and will of God

saints—people whom God has declared righteous; Christians

salvation—the free gift of the righteous God acting in grace toward the undeserving sinner who, by the gift of faith, trusts in the righteousness of Christ who has redeemed him by his death and justified him by his resurrection (*New Bible Dictionary* by J. D. Douglas, p. 1127)

sanctified—set apart to become more and more like Christ; holy

saved—given salvation

transformed—changed in character to be like Christ through the work of the Holy Spirit

uncircumcised—not having received the rite of circumcision, therefore separated from God's covenant with Abraham; non-Jew; Gentile

SUMMARY OF SCRIPTURE QUOTATIONS

I am not ashamed of the gospel, because it is the power of God for the salvation of everyone who believes; first for the Jew, then for the Gentile. For in the gospel a righteousness from God is revealed, a righteousness that is by faith from first to last, just as it is written: "The righteous will live by faith."

—Romans 1:16–17.

No, a man is a Jew if he is one inwardly; and circumcision is circumcision of the heart, by the Spirit, not by the written code. Such a man's praise is not from men, but from God.

—Romans 2:29.

Therefore no one will be declared righteous in his sight by observing the law; rather, through the law we become conscious of sin. For all have sinned and fall short of the glory of God.

—Romans 3:20, 23.

The words "it was credited to him" were written not for him alone, but also for us, to whom God will credit righteousness—for us who believe in him who raised Jesus our Lord from the dead. He was delivered over to death for our sins and was raised to life for our justification.

—*Romans 4:23–25.*

Therefore, since we have been justified through faith, we have peace with God through our Lord Jesus Christ, through whom we have gained access by faith into this grace in which we now stand. And we rejoice in the hope of the glory of God. Not only so, but we also rejoice in our sufferings, because we know that suffering produces perseverance; perseverance, character; and character, hope. And hope does not disappoint us, because God has poured out his love into our hearts by the Holy Spirit, whom he has given us.

—*Romans 5:1–5.*

Do not offer the parts of your body to sin, as instruments of wickedness, but rather offer yourselves to God, as those who have been brought from death to life; and offer the parts of your body to him as instruments of righteousness. For sin shall not be your master, because you are not under law, but under grace.

—*Romans 6:13–14.*

For in my inner being I delight in God's law; but I see another law at work in the members of my body, waging war against the law of my mind and making me a prisoner of the law of sin at work within my members. What a wretched man I am! Who will rescue me from this body of death? Thanks be to God—through Jesus Christ our Lord!

—*Romans 7:22–25.*

The Spirit himself testifies with our spirit that we are God's children. Now if we are children, then we are heirs—heirs of God and co-heirs with Christ, if indeed we share in his sufferings in order that we may also share in his glory.

—Romans 8:16–17.

For I am convinced that neither death nor life, neither angels nor demons, neither the present nor the future, nor any powers, neither height nor depth, nor anything else in all creation, will be able to separate us from the love of God that is in Christ Jesus our Lord.

—Romans 8:38–39.

For he says to Moses,
"I will have mercy on whom I have mercy, and I will have compassion on whom I have compassion."

—Romans 9:15.

That if you confess with your mouth, "Jesus is Lord," and believe in your heart that God raised him from the dead, you will be saved. For it is with your heart that you believe and are justified, and it is with your mouth that you confess and are saved.

—Romans 10:9–10.

Oh, the depth of the riches of the wisdom
   and knowledge of God!
 How unsearchable his judgments,
 and his paths beyond tracing out!
"Who has known the mind of the Lord?
 Or who has been his counselor?"
"Who has ever given to God,
 that God should repay him?"

For from him and through him and to him are all things.
  To him be the glory forever! Amen.
                                        —*Romans 11:33–36.*

Therefore, I urge you, brothers, in view of God's mercy, to offer your bodies as living sacrifices, holy and pleasing to God—which is your spiritual worship. Do not conform any longer to the pattern of this world, but be transformed by the renewing of your mind. Then you will be able to test and approve what God's will is—his good, pleasing and perfect will.
                                        —*Romans 12:1–2.*

Everyone must submit himself to the governing authorities, for there is no authority except that which God has established. The authorities that exist have been established by God. Consequently, he who rebels against the authority is rebelling against what God has instituted, and those who do so will bring judgment on themselves.
                                        —*Romans 13:1–2.*

Do not destroy the work of God for the sake of food. All food is clean, but it is wrong for a man to eat anything that causes someone else to stumble. It is better not to eat meat or drink wine or to do anything else that will cause your brother to fall.
                                        —*Romans 14:20–21.*

Therefore I glory in Christ Jesus in my service to God.
                                        —*Romans 15:17*

BIBLIOGRAPHY

Bruce, F. F., *The Epistle of Paul to the Romans, an Introduction and Commentary*. Grand Rapids: Eerdmans, 1963.

Clark, Adam, *The New Testament . . . a Commentary and Critical Notes*, Vol. 2. Nashville: Abingdon-Cokesbury Press, 1814.

Douglas, J. D., *The New Bible Dictionary*. Grand Rapids: Eerdmans, 1962.

Godet, F., *Commentary on St. Paul's Epistle to the Romans*. New York: Funk & Wagnalls, 1883.

Guthrie, D.; Motyer, J. A.; Stibbs, A. M.; and Wiseman, D.J., *The New Bible Commentary*. Grand Rapids: Eerdmans, 1970.

Hodge, Charles, *A Commentary on Romans*. Carlisle, Pa.: The Banner of Truth Trust. First published 1835. Reprinted 1975.

Ridenour, Fritz, *How to be a Christian Without Being Religious*. Glendale, Calif.: Regal Books, 1967.

Sproul, R. C., *Objections Answered*. Glendale, Calif.: Regal Books, 1978.

Steele, David N. and Thomas, Curtis C., *Romans, an Interpretative Outline*. Philadelphia: The Presbyterian and Reformed Publishing Company, 1963.

Stott, John R. W., *Men Made New, an Exposition of Romans 5–8*. Downers Grove, Ill.: InterVarsity Press, 1966.

Wilson, Geoffrey B., *Romans a Digest of Reformed Comment*. Carlisle, Pa.: The Banner of Truth Trust, 1976.

Wesley, John; Clark, Adam; Henry, Matthew; and others. *One Volume New Testament Commentary*. Grand Rapids: Baker Book House, 1972. Previously printed under the title *The Methodist Commentary on the New Testament*. London, 1893.